Published by Cypress Hills Press
Brooklyn, New York

Book design: Richard Tackett
http://www.richtackett.com

MAIGRET:
THE SERIES

BY

SCOTT V. PALMER

3

INTRODUCTION

This is a reference book about the British-made television series *Maigret*, which starred Michael Gambon and was show from 1992-93. It includes all twelve episodes in date order, numerous photographs, complete cast listings, and directorial credits.

There are also seven other films included; the 1949 film *The Man On the Eiffel Tower*, starring Charles Laughton as Maigret; *Maigret & the Lost Life* starring Basil Sydney (the pilot for the Rupert Davies series); *Maigret's Little Joke*-the last of the Davies series; and *Maigret*, starring Richard Harris.

I have also included the four feature-length made for television films made in 2016 and 2017 starring Rowan Atkinson as Maigret. The focus of the book however is on the series starring Sir Michael Gambon.

The series was filmed in Budapest, Hungary, and was produced by Jonathan Alwyn and Paul Marcus for Granada Television and distributed by ITV. It was shown on PBS in the United States on the Mystery programme. Each episode was approximately 50 minutes long.

Aside from Gambon (brilliantly cast as Maigret), regulars in the series included Geoffrey Hutchings as Sergeant Lucas, Jack Galloway as Inspector Janvier, James Larkin as Inspector Lapointe, and John Moffatt as Comeliau. Madame Maigret was played by Ciaran Madden in the first series and Barbara Flynn in series two.

TABLE OF CONTENTS

THE MAN ON THE EIFFEL TOWER (1949)

DIRECTED BY Burgess Meredith, Charles Laughton, Irving Allen

CAST

Charles Laughton.......Inspector Jules Maigret
Franchot Tone....................Johann Radek
Burgess Meredith..............Joseph Huertin
Robert Hutton...........................Bill Kirby
Patricia Roc...........................Helen Kirby
Jean Wallace........................Edna Wallace
Wilfrid Hyde-White.......Professor Grollet
Belita Gisella.................................Huertin
George Thorpe...........................Comelieu
William Phipps..............................Janvier
William Cottrell..............................Moers
Howard Vernon...........................Inspector
Chaz Chase.....................................Waiter

Charles Laughton

Franchot Tone

Burgess Meredith

Robert Hutton

Patricia Roc

Jean Wallace

Wilfrid Hyde-White

Belita Gisella

George Thorpe

97 minutes

William Phipps

William Cottrell

Howard Vernon

Chaz Chase

In Paris, Bill Kirby, a dandy living off his aunt, wishes her dead in public and catches the ear of Johann Radek, a desperate down and out medical student fellow who is very clever but also a bit crazy.

6

Radek is paid by Kirby to murder his wealthy aunt. That way Kirby can get his inheritance, pay off his wife to divorce him, and marry his wife's friend.

Joseph Huertin, a knife grinder and would-be burglar stumbles upon the corpses of the old lady and her maid. Heurtin, who is almost legally blind, loses his glasses and must be helped home by the killer.

Foreign Film Poster

Film Poster

Charles Laughton, George Thorpe

Wilfrid Hyde-White as the Professor

Robert Hutton, Charles Laughton

Franchot Tone on the Eiffel Tower

On the night of the murder, Inspector Maigret is assigned to the case and quickly tracks down the owner of the thick glasses. Heurtin helps identify Radek, but there is no real evidence against him.

The police and Maigret are led on chases through the streets and over the rooftops of Paris and finally up the girders of the Eiffel Tower. Radek keeps taunting the police until they realize that he is the killer.

One reviewer stated "The film plays like Hitchcock. It uses the old stand-by plot of an innocent man wanted for murder and a famous landmark figure into the finale."

Another said "Probably most impressive in this film are the performances. The top-of-the-line acting cast includes Burgess Meredith, the always amazing Charles Laughton, as well as Franchot Tone.

Film Poster

Film Poster

Charles Laughton, Burgess Meredith

Charles Laughton as Maigret

Robert Hutton, Jean Wallace and Patricia Roc are fascinating additions to this storyline. The dysfunctional characters leap off the screen, contributing heavily to the unique feel of this movie.

Note sent to the police

Maigret enters the scene

Charles Laughton looks intense

Wilfrid Hyde-White, Charles Laughton

William Cottrell, Charles Laughton

Belita, Burgess Meredith

Franchot Tone is particularly interesting as Johann Radek, a disgraced medical student. Tone has a wide-eyed look to him which lends itself incredibly well to a particular sense of unhinged menacing.

In the narrative, Radek is a former medical student with a promising background. However, his career is tainted by manic-depressive episodes leading to his dark proclivities.

The film's final sequence makes fascinating use of not only the movie's Parisian setting, but the Eiffel Tower. The chase sequence is tightly edited and tense. Few films have duplicated a scene like this before or since."

William Cottrell, Charles Laughton

Charles Laughton, Wilfrid Hyde-White

Maigret discusses the case

Charles Laughton as Inspector Maigret

Robert Hutton, Jean Wallace

MAIGRET & THE LOST LIFE (1959)

DIRECTED BY Campbell Logan

CAST

Basil Sydney.................Inspector Maigret
Henry Oscar...................................Lognon
Andre Van Gyseghem....................Janvier
Mary Merrall...............Madame Cremieux
Philip Guard.....................................Lucas
Anne Blake....................Madame Maigret
Marian Spencer..............Madame Laboine
Grace Arnold.................Madame Lognon
Michael Brennan..............................Feret
Jane Henderson................................Irene
Patrick Troughton........Albert the Barman
Gordon Sterne................................Clark
Margot Van Der Burgh..............Concierge
David Lander................................Santoni
Allan McClelland..........................Doctor
Helen Misener............Madamoiselle Pore
Gillian Vaughan.............................Jeanine
Christopher Steele..........................Waiter
Andre Maranne...........................Croupier
Stella Riley.......................................Rose
Louis Raynes.............................Gendarme
Lillian Moubrey..........Woman at Window

AND: Leslie Glazer, Wilfred Grove, Ivor
Kimmel, Joseph Levine, Benn Simons

Basil Sydney   Henry Oscar   Andre Van Gyseghem

Mary Merrall   Philip Guard   Anne Blake

Marian Spencer   Grace Arnold   Michael Brennan

Jane Henderson   Patrick Troughton   Gordon Sterne

Margot Van Der Burgh   David Lander   Allan McClelland

Helen Misener   Gillian Vaughan   Christopher Steele   Andre Maranne

75 minutes

This dramatization was presented on the B.B.C. Sunday Night Theatre. It aired on April 12, 1959, starring Basil Sydney as Maigret. This was a pilot episode for the series which was produced by the B.B.C. and ran from 1960-63, starring Rupert Davies as Maigret, which included 52 episodes-which the B.B.C. supposedly has in its archives.

Giles Cooper (1918-1966), a former stage actor, adapted the story for the B.B.C. Cooper wrote screenplays and television adaptations for nearly 100 television productions-including about 20 of the series starring Rupert Davies.

He also adapted many B.B.C. and I.T.V. productions, including two series of Sherlock Holmes, as well as classics like Epitaph For a Spy, Madame Bovary, For Whom the

Bell Tolls, A Farewell to Arms, and Les Miserables.

The distinguished actor Basil Sydney (1894-1968) played Maigret here. Sydney was a successful actor of both the London and Broadway stages, and appeared in more than 60 films, many of them classic of their time.

He was ably supported by veteran actors like Henry Oscar, Andre Van Gyseghem, Mary Merrall, and Patrick Troughton, the latter of whom would find TV fame as Doctor Who.

No print of this production appears to be available, nevertheless its inclusion is warranted in that it was an important landmark in launching a series that was greatly received (at one point the series was getting 15 million viewers).

14

MAIGRET'S LITTLE JOKE (1963)

DIRECTED BY Terence Williams

CAST

Rupert Davies......Chief Inspector Maigret
Ewen Solon......................Inspector Lucas
Helen Shingler...............Madame Maigret
Neville Jason...............................Lapointe
Michael Goodliffe......................Dr. Javet
Neil McCallum.........................Dr. Negrel
Stephanie Bidmead.........Antoinette Vidal
Barry Letts.....................................Gaston
Anne Robson....................................Marie
Lucy Young....................Martine Chapuis
Constance Wake..................Evelyne Javet
Ann Way.....................................Concierge
Shelagh Fraser.................Claire Jusserand

Rupert Davies

Ewen Solon

Helen Shingler

Neville Jason

Michael Goodliffe

Neil McCallum

Stephanie Bidmead

Barry Letts

Anne Robson

Lucy Young

Constance Wake

Ann Way

Shelagh Fraser

Pepito Moreno

Maigret is at home with an injured shoulder; he is visited by Lucas, who has just been promoted to inspector. The two men talk about a recent case, where a police sergeant was killed.

15

Madame Maigret wants her husband to take things easy and forget all about work. Lucas gets a call, and has to leave to attend to a case-it may be murder.

Lucas arrives at the surgery of Dr. Javet to find that Madame Javet is dead on the bed-naked. Dr. Negrel says she has been dead for two days. Cause of death was heart failure.

Rupert Davies on the phone

Ewen Solon, Neil McCallum

Ewen Solon as Inspector Lucas

Rupert Davies looking surprised

TV Ident

Lucy Young, Rupert Davies

Helen Shingler, Rupert Davies

Maigret lights his pipe

Rupert Davies, Ewen Solon

Madame was supposedly on holiday with her husband-nobody knew she returned. That is, if she left in the first place. Javet returns and says his wife was supposed to go to St. Tropez to visit a friend.

17

Javet tells Lucas that his wife suffered from having an abnormally slow pulse, so her death was not a complete surprise to him. Lucas tells the doctor that the autopsy showed Madame Javet had digitalis in her system.

Shelagh Fraser, Michael Goodliffe

Rupert Davies, Barry Letts

Constance Wake, Michael Goodliffe

Michael Goodliffe, Ewen Solon

Lucy Young, Rupert Davies

Ewen Solon, Neil McCallum

Maigret meanwhile is approached by a woman named Martine Chapuis, who is the girlfriend of Dr. Negrel. Although he is supposed to be resting, Maigret decides to do his own investigating.

Thanks to Maigret, Lucas solves the case. And yes, it was murder. Maigret receives a card after Lucas pays a call; it seems that the new Inspector knew all the time about Maigret and his involvement!

Lucy Young, Rupert Davies

Ann Way, Rupert Davies

Ewen Solon, Neville Jason, Ann Way

Neville Jason, Ewen Solon

Michael Goodliffe, Stephanie Bidmead, Ewen Solon

MAIGRET (1988)

DIRECTED BY Paul Lynch

CAST

Richard Harris......Inspector Jules Maigret
Patrick O'Neal..................Kevin Portman
Victoria Tennant.............Victoria Portman
Ian Ogilvy.........................Daniel Portman
Barbara Shelley.................Louise Maigret
Dominique Barnes...............Tara Portman
Eric Deacon........................Tony Portman
Richard Durden....................Julian Braden
Andrew McCulloch...........Sergeant Lucas
Annette Andre..............Judith Hollenbeck
Caroline Munro....................Carolyn Page
Milo Sperber.......................Oliver Durbin
Vernon Dobtcheff..........................Gannett
Don Henderson...................Barge Captain
John Abineri................................Renault
Mark Audley.....................................Ekers
Eve Ferret..............................Mrs. Tippet
Adrian Cairns...........................Dr. Parton
Lachele Carl...............Sgt. Leila Normand

Richard Harris   Patrick O'Neal   Victoria Tennant

Ian Ogilvy   Barbara Shelley   Dominique Barnes

Eric Deacon   Richard Durden   Andrew McCulloch

Annette Andre   Caroline Munro   Milo Sperber

Vernon Dobtcheff   Don Henderson   John Abineri   Mark Audley   Eve Ferret   Adrian Cairns   Lachele Carl

| Mourner | Ship's Doctor | Ship's Officer | Thief | Train Conductor | Train Steward |

94 minutes

Reclusive industrialist Kevin Portman shows up in Paris. Meanwhile on a train, a man named Oliver Durbin has written a letter, which he hides under a seat. When the ticket collector knocks on the door, Durbin opens it-and is shot to death.

Television Poster

Richard Harris as Maigret

Barbara Shelley, Richard Harris

Later Durbin's body is found floating in the river-he was apparently thrown from the train. Chief Inspector Maigret is soon on the case; Durbin had one been a policeman, but had been kicked off the force.

After his dismissal, Durbin worked as a private investigator. Apparently he was on a very important case. The envelope he hid was found on the train; it contained a number of photo negatives.

Richard Harris, Andrew McCulloch

Victoria Tennant, Ian Ogilvy

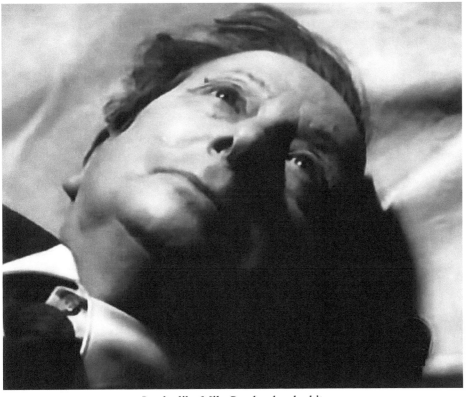
Looks like Milo Sperber has had it

23

When Maigret has them developed, he notices they are pictures of Kevin Portman. Maigret calls on Portman's son Daniel, who denies knowing Durbin.

However the name of William Hollenbeck, Daniel's assistant, was found in an appointment calendar belonging to Durbin. It turns out that Daniel was on the same train with Durbin-he says it was merely a coincidence.

Maigret holds up the victim's shoe

Dominique Barnes and her horse

Patrick O'Neal as Kevin Portman

Barbara Shelley, Richard Harris

Victoria Tennant, Richard Harris

Richard Harris as Inspector Maigret

Hollenbeck is apparently in London on a conference; his wife is not too helpful to Maigret concerning his exact whereabouts. After Maigret puts out an A.P.B., Hollenbeck's car is found-with his body in the trunk.

When a man falls off a roof to his death after stealing a letter Durbin wrote, Maigret concentrates on the entire Portman family-all of whom are lying to him about things.

Richard Harris, Don Henderson

Barbara Shelley as Madame Maigret

Patrick O'Neal, Ship's Officer

Dominique Barnes, Victoria Tennant, Ian Ogilvy, Eric Deacon, Patrick O'Neal

Victoria Tennant, Dominique Barnes

Patrick O'Neal being questioned

Sultrry looking Caroline Munro

Kevin Portman wants to take complete control of the family business; his son Tony is agreeable, but Daniel Portman has other ideas. They all go for a cruise; Maigret and his wife are also on board. Soon, someone tries to kill Maigret by pushing him down stairs.

After Daniel's wife Victoria is murdered, Maigret has three crimes to solve-all connected with the Portmans. Maigret discovers the real Kevin Portman is dead; an imposter took his place, and also killed Durbin and Hollenbeck. Tony Portman killed Victoria however; motive: greed.

Mrs. Hollenbeck at the morgue

Caroline Munro, Richard Durden

Eve Ferret, Richard Harris

THE PATIENCE OF MAIGRET SEASON 1 EPISODE 1

DIRECTED BY James Cellan Jones ORIGINAL AIR DATE: 2/9/92

CAST

Michael Gambon..Inspector Jules Maigret
Ciaran Madden...............Madame Maigret
Geoffrey Hutchings...........Sergeant Lucas
Jack Galloway................Inspector Janvier
James Larkin...............Inspector Lapointe
Ann Todd.......................................Josette
John Moffatt...............................Comeliau
Cheryl Campbell.................Aline Bauche
Trevor Peacock...............Manuel Palmari
Greg Hicks....................Fernand Barillard
Rachel Fielding...........Madame Barillard
Matyelok Gibbs.......................Concierge
Robert McBain.....................James Stuart
Janos Gosztonyi........................Jeff Claes
Christian Rodska...........................Moers
Ron Cook.....................................Pernelle
Robert Kovacs...............................Louis
Paul Bigley.....................................Waiter
Henry Goodman...................Hotel Porter
Sandor Reisenbuchler..............Policeman
Agi Soproni.............................Prostitute

Michael Gambon Ciaran Madden Geoffrey Hutchings

Jack Galloway James Larkin Ann Todd

John Moffatt Cheryl Campbell Trevor Peacock

Greg Hicks Rachel Fielding Matyelok Gibbs

Robert McBain Janos Gosztonyi Christian Rodska

| Ron Cook | Robert Kovacs | Paul Bigley | Henry Goodman | Bartender | Boy | Policeman |

Three men rob a jewelry store, smashing the windows and driving away. Comeliau tells Maigret that there have been more than 70 robberies over the last seven years- none solved. Maigret believe Manuel Palmeri is behind it.

Underneath bridge view of the river

Rachel Fielding, Michael Gambon

Ann Todd in her apartment

TV Poster

Ciaran Madden, Michael Gambon

James Larkin, Michael Gambon

Michael Gambon, James Larkin

Trevor Peacock, Michael Gambon

Manuel Palmeri is a master jewel thief confined to his Paris apartment in a wheelchair. Despite his record, Maigret has a fondness for the criminal and after he is found shot to death, the murder investigation becomes his top priority.

When the Chief Inspector discovers that the venerable apartment building is owned covertly by Palmari's mistress, he is convinced that the solution to both crimes lies among the surviving tenants of the building.

31

They compose a very eccentric group that includes a deaf-and-dumb Belgian model maker, a gossipy elderly woman with a penchant for parrots, a flashy but unpleasant salesman, and a cantankerous concierge.

Geoffrey Hutchings, Cherie Lunghi

Geoffrey Hutchings, James Larkin

Michael Gambon as Inspector Maigret

At a restaurant, Maigret, accompanied by Inspector Lapoine, discovers the owner has already heard about the death of Palmeri, even though it has not yet been in the newspapers.

After a second murder, which seems senseless, Maigret comes up with the solution to both crimes. Maigret isn't happy with the result; he says he much prefers the company of elderly gangsters.

John Moffatt looking serious

Jack Galloway with the chalkboard

Boy with toy gun

Trevor Peacock, Michael Gambon

Jack Galloway, Michael Gambon

TV Poster

Matyelok Gibbs, Michael Gambon

Michael Gambon, Geoffrey Hutchings

Geoffrey Hutchings, Cherie Lunghi

When he meets Comeliau, he gives him two possible theories of the killer, and leaves it up to the prosecutor. Madame Maigret says to her husband that he really knows what happened. But Maigret says "No one ever knows what really happened."

DIRECTED BY John Glenister ORIGINAL AIR DATE: 2/16/92

CAST

Michael Gambon..Inspector Jules Maigret
Ciaran Madden..............Madame Maigret
Geoffrey Hutchings...........Sergeant Lucas
Jack Galloway................Inspector Janvier
James Larkin...............Inspector Lapointe
John Moffatt.............................Comeliau
Christopher Benjamin.....Guillaume Serre
Margery Withers...............Madame Serre
Sandy Ratcliff..........Ernestine Jussiaume
John Gill.............................Dr. Dutilleux
Merelina Kendall.........................Eugenie
Vilma Hollingbery.....................Landlady
Gooey Law.......................Builder's Clerk
Raymond Mason...............Man With Dog
Jane Slavin................................Waitress
Zoltan Gera....................................Waiter
Antal Leisen..........................Sad Freddie

Michael Gambon   Ciaran Madden   Geoffrey Hutchings

Jack Galloway   James Larkin   John Moffatt

Christopher Benjamin Margery Withers   Sandy Ratcliff

John Gill   Merelina Kendall Vilma Hollingbery

Gooey Law   Raymond Mason   Jane Slavin   Antal Leisen

Maigret is visited by Ernestine, the wife of a burglar known as Sad Freddie. Whilst breaking into a house he discovered a body and is so alarmed he has fled the country.

It seems that Maigret once tried to arrest Ernestine-many years ago-and she took off all her clothes and refused to move. Maigret called Lucas and Janvier, who brought some blankets.

Geoffrey Hutchings, Gooey Law

Michael Gambon, John Gill

Michael Gambon as Maigret

Michael Gambon, Geoffrey Hutchings

Christopher Benjamin, Michael Gambon

Christopher Benjamin looks intense

The trail leads Maigret to a dentist who lives with his domineering elderly mother. His wife has gone missing but Maigret needs to find a body if he is to provide a link.

Upon arriving at the home of Guilliaume Serre, the dentist, Maigret asks to examine the safe-which was installed eighteen years previously by Sad Freddie.

Maigret realizes, as usual, that everyone is lying about something. Madame Maigret suggest Freddie, the burglar, may have been the killer but Maigret says Freddie isn't the killing type.

Christopher Benjamin, Margery Withers

Margery Withers as Madame Serre

Geoffrey Hutchings looking nonplussed

Michael Gambon, Geoffrey Hutchings

Merelina Kendall, Geoffrey Hutchings

Geoffrey Hutchings, Christopher Benjamin

Jane Slavin, Michael Gambon, James Larkin

Michael Gambon, James Larkin

Geoffrey Hutchings, Jack Galloway

Michael Gambon, James Larkin

James Larkin, Michael Gambon

After a search of Serre's house, Maigret has the dentist brought to headquarters for questioning. Serre insist that his wife is not dead-she is merely away-supposedly in Holland.

Maigret discovers that Serre's father was a drinker, womanizer, and roué in general, which lead to his early death. Madame Serre did not want her son to end up the same way as his father; she gives Maigret her confession.

Suitcase pulled from the river

Michael Gambon with John Gill

Geoffrey Hutchings as Lucas

MAIGRET GOES TO SCHOOL SEASON 1 EPISODE 3

DIRECTED BY James Cellan Jones ORIGINAL AIR DATE: 2/23/92

CAST

Michael Gambon..Inspector Jules Maigret
Geoffrey Hutchings...........Sergeant Lucas
Jack Galloway................Inspector Janvier
Struan Rodger.....................Joseph Gastin
Joanna David....................Madame Gastin
Max Beazley...................Jean-Paul Gastin
Jim Norton...........................Dr. Bresselles
Adrian Lukis.................Captain Danielou
Godfrey James.................Louis Paumelle
Pip Donaghy..............................Marcellin
Eve Saabo...................Madame Marcellin
Guy Faulkner..............Philippe Marcellin
Jamie Fletcher Lawson.......Marcel Sellier
Kati Marton......................Maria Smelker
Istvan Hunyadkirthy...........Theo Coumart
Laszlo Kiss.................Temporary Teacher
Agi Csere.....................................Waitress

Michael Gambon   Geoffrey Hutchings   Jack Galloway

Struan Rodger   Joanna David   Max Beazley

Jim Norton   Adrian Lukis   Godfrey James

Pip Donaghy   Eve Saabo   Guy Faulkner

Jamie Fletcher Lawson   Kati Marton   Istvan Hunyadkirthy   Laszlo Kiss   M. Sellier   Priest   Station Master

Maigret is called to investigate a murder in a small village near to La Rochelle, the victim being old Jeanne, shot through her window. She was the local post mistress with access to everyone's mail.

Joseph Gastin, the schoolteacher, comes to Paris and asks for the help of Maigret. But the Inspector is out, so he tells his story to Inspector Janvier and Sergeant Lucas. But Maigret returns and decides to investigate.

TV Poster

Jim Norton pouring some tea

Maigret looks at a clue

Joanna David standing in her yard

Train stopped at the station

42

The main suspect is the married schoolteacher, but the local doctor explains to Maigret that this is chiefly because he has come from Paris and the villagers resent newcomers. Maigret meets resistance from almost all the villagers; even Gastin's own son does not want to speak to him. He gets better results however when he interviews some of the schoolboys.

Struan Rodger, Michael Gambon

Godfrey James, Michael Gambon

Geoffrey Hutchings, Jack Galloway, Michael Gambon

Adrian Lukis, Michael Gambon   Jim Norton, Michael Gambon

Michael Gambon, Guy Faulkner

During Maigret's investigation, Gastin is formerly arrested, due primarily to one of his pupils coming forward and saying he saw Gastin leave a shed at the dead woman's house near to the time of the murder.

Maigret gets a further clue when he investigates a motorbike accident that involved young Philippe Marcellin. The accident was the boy's fault, but he let it be thought that the driver was at fault so his father could collect insurance money.

Max Beazley, Michael Gambon

Michael Gambon, Guy Faulkner

Adrian Lukis with a flower

Godfrey James, Istvan Hunyadkirthy,
Michael Gambon

Kati Marton, Michael Gambon

Michael Gambon looking in

It turns out thay the dead woman saw the boy, and started shooting at him. He took a shot at the window, hoping to frighten the obnoxious woman. But he missed; he put the rifle in the shed, where his father found it, and shot the woman. Maigret tells Philippe that his father will go to prison-but not for very long.

Michael Gambon, Struan Rodger

Adrian Lukis and policemen

Godfrey James, Pip Donaghy, Michael Gambon

DIRECTED BY John Glenister ORIGINAL AIR DATE: 3/1/92

CAST

Michael Gambon..Inspector Jules Maigret
Ciaran Madden...............Madame Maigret
Geoffrey Hutchings...........Sergeant Lucas
Jack Galloway................Inspector Janvier
James Larkin...............Inspector LaPointe
Marjorie Sommerville....Madame Antoine
Frances Cuka....................Angele Louette
Mark Lockyer....................Emile Louette
Mark Frankel................................Marcel
Harold Innocent..............Pepito Giovanni
Zoe Hodges...............................Little Girl
Tricia Vincent.....................Girl's Mother
Andras Ambrus...............................Caille
Ferenc Nemethy........................Old Man
Sandor Tery........................Police Driver

Michael Gambon   Ciaran Madden   Geoffrey Hutchings

Jack Galloway   James Larkin   Marjorie Sommerville

Frances Cuka   Mark Lockyer   Mark Frankel

Harold Innocent   Zoe Hodges   Tricia Vincent

Madame Antoine, an elderly widow, is sure someone is following her and entering her flat when she's away. Maigret assumes she is having delusions and assigns a subordinate to escort her home.

Ferenc Nemethy   Sandor Tery

47

When the woman is found smothered to death, the detective is plagued with guilt and vows to apprehend her killer. The only suspects are her only relatives: her middle-aged niece Angele, Angele's paid gigolo, and her wastrel son who sponged off the victim.

Marjorie Sommerville,
Geoffrey Hutchings

Television Poster

TV Poster

Marjorie Sommerville as Madame Antoine

Michael Gambon, Geoffrey Hutchings

Frances Cuka, James Larkin

Geoffrey Hutchings scratching his head

Maigret reckons since the old lady was killed at home, the murderer must have been looking for something. Maigret only hopes the killer did not find it.

Angele Louette, the niece, seems to be heiress to Madame Antione's property; Maigret asks her why she keeps a gun in the house; she says after all her aunt was not shot.

Her lover Marcel is also keeping company with a notorious gangster; this does not especially worry An-gele. Marcel appears also to have been in Madame Antoine's apart-ment. He denies it however.

Michael Gambon, Ciaran Madden

Geoffrey Hutchings, Michael Gambon

Mark Lockyer playing guitar

When Marcel's dead body is fished out of the river the next day-the victim of a knifing-Sergeant Lucas tells Maigret that "At least it saves us the cost of a trial."

Angele says that yes, it was Marcel who suffocated her aunt; she loved him and didn't want to let Maigret know what he had done. She also didn't tell Maigret where she was at the time.

Body fished out of the river

Michael Gambon, Ciaran Madden

Michael Gambon as Maigret

Michael Gambon, Marjorie Sommerville

Michael Gambon, Ciaran Madden

Maigret on the telephone

Michael Gambon & James Larkin

The Madwoman appears to be dead

Harold Innocent, Michael Gambon

James Larkin, Michael Gambon

Maigret has solved the case but blames himself, for want of having done things differently. "Both deaths are my responsibility," he tells Madame Maigret.

MAIGRET ON HOME GROUND SEASON 1 EPISODE 5

DIRECTED BY James Cellan Jones ORIGINAL AIR DATE: 3/8/92

CAST

Michael Gambon..Inspector Jules Maigret
Geoffrey Hutchings...........Sergeant Lucas
John Warnaby....................Count Maurice
James Clyde.........................Jean Metayer
Gareth Thomas............................Gautier

Michael Gambon   Geoffrey Hutchings   John Warnaby

Paul Brightwell...................Emile Gautier
Eva Orkenyi...................Madame Gautier
Daniel Moynihan.................Father Martin
Jonathan Adams...............Dr. Bouchardon
Sue Withers....................Madame Bonnet

James Clyde   Gareth Thomas   Paul Brightwell

Sebastian Knapp.................Ernest Bonnet
Charlotte Mitchell.................Marie-Tatin
Charles Taylor-Coutts.................Sacristan
Sandor Szabo.............Print Shop Foreman
Flora Kadar.........................Flower Seller

Eva Orkenyi   Daniel Moynihan   Jonathan Adams

Sandor Korospataki.........................Albert
Miklos Hajdu..............................Chauffer
Agi Margitay..............................Countess

Sue Withers   Sebastian Knapp   Charlotte Mitchell

Charles Taylor-Coutts   Flora Kadar   Sandor Korospataki   Miklos Hajdu   Agi Margitay   Printer

Maigret receives an anonymous note announcing that a crime will be committed during first mass at the rural church in his provincial home town.

Unable to resist the temptation, the detective attends the service and finds that the countess whom his late father worked for as bailiff has died from a heart attack.

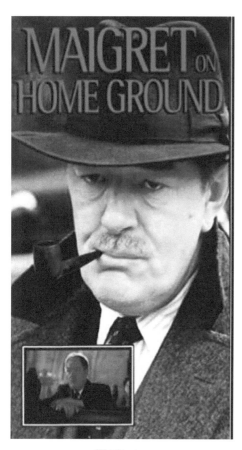

TV Poster

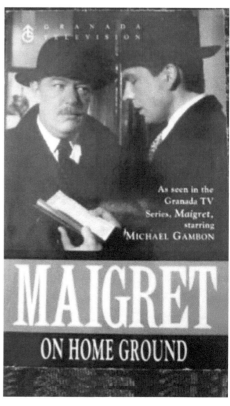

Television Poster

Jonathan Adams, Michael Gambon

John Warnaby as Count Maurice

Maigret meets the current bailiff, a man named Gautier, who has a wife and a son named Emile. Maigret encounters Emile and his mother in the cemetery, where Maigret was visiting his father's grave.

When he discovers that a bogus news article falsely announcing her son's suicide in her prayer book, Maigret correctly assumes that foul play was involved.

Fishing on the lake

Maigret pours some green stuff

Maigret with his trademark pipe

John Warnaby, Gareth Thomas

Maigret discovers the dead woman

Maigret lights his pipe

Maigret questions Father Martin, who says that he hid the prayer book. When Maigret wants to know why, the priest won't tell him; he says it involves the sacred right of the confession.

People keep either lying outright to Maigret, or neglecting to tell him things. The countess's son, and Jean Metayer both hate each other, but Maigret tells them that neither one of them is guilty.

Flora Kadar, Michael Gambon

Michael Gambon, Daniel Moynihan, John Warnaby

Flora Kadar, Michael Gambon

Michael Gambon, Charles Taylor-Coutts,
Jonathan Adams

John Warnaby, Michael Gambon

Geoffrey Hutchings, Michael Gambon

Michael Gambon, Charlotte Mitchell

Eva Orkenyi, Paul Brightwell

Jonathan Adams, Paul Brightwell

Gautier, the bailiff, has been stealing from the countess; his son Emile was the one that sent the countess the newspaper clipping. He sent Maigret the letter because he wanted to be caught. He had a terrible guilt complex. Maigret takes him away.

MAIGRET SETS A TRAP SEASON 1 EPISODE 6

DIRECTED BY John Glenister ORIGINAL AIR DATE: 3/15/92

CAST

Michael Gambon..Inspector Jules Maigret
Ciaran Madden...............Madame Maigret
Geoffrey Hutchings...........Sergeant Lucas
Jack Galloway................Inspector Janvier
James Larkin...............Inspector Lapointe
John Moffatt..............................Comeliau
Ann Mitchell..................Madame Moncin
Richard Willis..................Marcel Moncin
Leonie Mellinger.............Yvonne Moncin
Catherine Russell..........Marthe Jesserand
Christian Rodska.............................Moers
Jonathan Tafler..............................Rougin
Charlotte Barker...........................Maguy
Dora Farkas.....................................Odile

Michael Gambon   Ciaran Madden   Geoffrey Hutchings

Jack Galloway   James Larkin   John Moffatt

Ann Mitchell   Richard Willis   Leonie Mellinger

Catherine Russell   Christian Rodska   Jonathan Tafler

Charlotte Barker   Dora Farkas

A serial killer is murdering young women in Paris. The press is giving Maigret a hard time. Maigret thinks the killer is a maniac. The victims appear to have nothing in common.

Examination of some cloth found at a crime scene proves that the material was not made in France-it was English. Maigret gets a list of all the English cloth suppliers.

Michael Gambon & John Moffatt

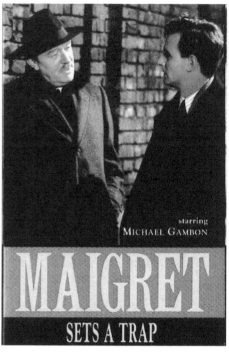

Television Poster

Catherine Russell, Michael Gambon

Michael Gambon as Jules Maigret

Maigret at his desk

James Larkin, Michael Gambon

TV Poster

Maigret with some suspects

Richard Willis, Michael Gambon

Maigret sets a trap using a police-woman as a decoy in the murder location. The killer attacks her but when the police come he runs away, leaving a clue which links to Marcel Moncin, a married mother's boy.

Maigret arrests Moncin but while he is in custody there is another killing. When Maigret and Janvier question Moncin's mother, she tells him her son wouldn't hurt a fly.

Has Maigret got the wrong man or does Moncin have an accomplice? Maigret talks to Marcel, trying to find out the relationships he had with his father and mother.

Christian Rodska, Michael Gambon

Michael Gambon, Jack Galloway

James Larkin, Leonie Mellinger

He is sure that Moncin is crazy; he even tells him that he will wind up in a lunatic asylum. He says that he is not insane; his wife and mother tell Maigret to release Marcel.

Evidence under the microscope

Jonathan Tafler, Michael Gambon

Leonie Mellinger as Yvonne Moncin

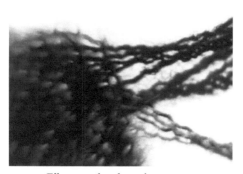
Fibers under the microscope

Richard Willis, James Larkin

Michael Gambon, Jack Galloway

Sign Maigret was searching for

Jonathan Tafler, Charlotte Barker

Finally, Moncin admits that he killed the women; nobody, he says, thought that he was capable of being a murderer. Moncin's wife admits to killing the other woman while her husband was in jail. She seems to take satisfaction that she, not Madame Moncin, tried to help Marcel.

DIRECTED BY John Strickland ORIGINAL AIR DATE: 3/14/93

CAST

Michael Gambon..Inspector Jules Maigret
Geoffrey Hutchings...........Sergeant Lucas
Jack Galloway................Inspector Janvier
James Larkin...............Inspector Lapointe
Minnie Driver................................Arlette
Tony Doyle....................................Freddie
Michael Sheen...........................Philippe
Brenda Blethyn.................................Rose
Michael Billington.........................Oscar
Sandor Szabo..............................Jeweler
Sandor Korospataky.....................Doctor
Laura Cox................................Concierge
Zoltan Korospataky.................Policeman
Jaye Griffiths....................................Tania
Clara Salaman..................................Betty
Jill Freud........................Madame Trochau
Janet Dale..................Madame Mancouer

Michael Gambon   Geoffrey Hutchings   Jack Galloway

James Larkin   Minnie Driver   Tony Doyle

Michael Sheen   Brenda Blethyn   Michael Billington

Sandor Szabo   Sandor Korospataky   Laura Cox

Zoltan Korospataky   Clara Salaman   Jill Freud   Janet Dale

Arlette, a beautiful but alcoholic stripper in a sleazy club, comes forward to police to report overhearing a murder plot at the club targeting a countess.

Shortly thereafter her testimony becomes inconsistent, and she recants it. But not too long afterwards, she is found murdered; also murdered is the countess, whose death Arlette predicted.

Michael Gambon, Geoffrey Hutchings, Zoltan Korospataki

Michael Gambon, Brenda Blethyn, Tony Doyle

Maigret arrives at the scene

When Maigret investigates her colourful private life, he discovers the club owner as well as one of his valued assistants, Inspector Albert Lapointe, among her most ardent admirers.

Lapointe tells Maigret that he began seeing Arlette about three weeks before she was murdered; he soon fell hard for her. He was with her that night, but did not hear any murder plot at the next table as Arlette had stated.

Michael Gambon as Maigret

Michael Gambon, Tony Doyle

Michael Gambon, Geoffrey Hutchings

Michael Gambon, James Larkin

Michael Gambon, Clara Salaman

Geoffrey Hutchings as Lucas

Lapointe blames Maigret for not protecting Arlette; he tells the Chief Inspector that if he does not find the bastard that murdered her, he will do so himself.

At first, Maigret tells Lapointe to take a week off, but Lapointe says he must remain on the case. Maigret lets him, telling him to see if Lucas needs some help.

The investigation leads Maigret and the police through the seamy world of nightclubs, drug dealers and eventually leads to a man named Oscar, who Lapointe shoots dead.

Jack Galloway as Janvier

TV Poster

Looks like an important clue

Jack Galloway, Michael Gambon

Maigret and a nightclub hostess

Maigret in conference

Geoffrey Hutchings, Michael Gambon

Jill Freud, Michael Gambon

Maigret questions a witness

Tony Doyle, Michael Gambon

Jack Galloway, James Larkin

Lapointe has some regret at shooting Oscar-who was armed with a hostage, but Maigret doesn't. He says to Laponite, "What else cold you do-it's your job."

DIRECTED BY Nicholas Renton ORIGINAL AIR DATE: 3/21/93

CAST

Michael Gambon..Inspector Jules Maigret
Geoffrey Hutchings...........Sergeant Lucas
Jack Galloway................Inspector Janvier
James Larkin...............Inspector Lapointe
John Moffatt.............................Comeliau
Toyah Willcox....................................Gigi
Michael J. Shannon.............Oswald Clark
John Kavanagh....................Jean Ramuel
Michael J. Jackson.............Prosper Donge
Roger Hume..........................Colleboeuf
Clifford Rose.................................Jolivet
Charles Simon..........................Old Man
Nicola Duffet.............................Charlotte
Tibor Dalotti......................................Zebio
Polly Hemingway..........Madame Ramuel
Tony Mathews..................Hotel Manager
Ferenc Nemethy............................Doctor
Francine Brody..............Ellen Darrowman
Gergely Hegedus............................Teddy
Balazs Galko........................Taxi Driver
Bela Jaki............................Cannes Barman
Flora Kadar............................Nursemaid

Michael Gambon   Geoffrey Hutchings   Jack Galloway

James Larkin   John Moffatt   Toyah Willcox

Michael J. Shannon   John Kavanagh   Michael J. Jackson

Roger Hume   Clifford Rose   Charles Simon

Nicola Duffet   Polly Hemingway   Tony Mathews

| Ferenc Nemethy | Francine Brody | Gergely Hegedus | Bela Jaki | Flora Kadar | Injured Man | Newspaper Seller |

Mimi Clark, the beautiful wife of American businessman Oswald Clark is found strangled in a kitchen locker in the posh Majestic Hotel in Paris.

Her body is found early in the morning, in a locker in the kitchen cloakroom, by the breakfast cook, Prosper Donge.

Geoffrey Hutchings, Michael J. Shannon

Bela Jaki, Michael Gambon

Michael Gambon as Maigret

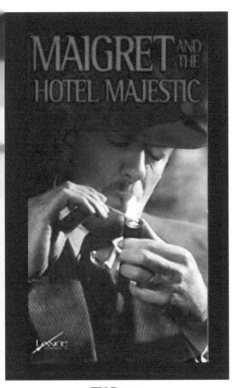

TV Poster

Michael J. Shannon, John Moffatt

Michael Gambon, Geoffrey Hutchings

Charles Simon, Michael Gambon

Dead body on the floor

Maigret notes that the murdered woman arrived at her fatal meeting armed with a pistol and discovers that Clark is having an affair with his son's governess.

Oswald Clark said he had gone to Rome on business, but in fact spent the night in Paris with Ellen Darroman, his maid, and they stayed at a different hotel.

Maigret learns that Mimi Clark had been a hostess in Cannes, in a club called La Belle Étoile, where Charlotte, girlfriend of Donge worked. Donge also had worked in Cannes at the Miramar Hotel.

Maigret goes to Cannes to see Gigi, another dancer at the club, where he learns that Mimi had had Donge's son, but told her husband it was his. But even before he returns he learns that Donge has been arrested.

Nicola Duffett, Michael J. Jackson, Toyah Willcox, John Kavanagh

Tony Mathews, Michael Gambon

John Kavanagh, Polly Hemingway, Michael Gambon, Geoffrey Hutchings

While Maigret was gone, another murder occurred, that of Justin Colleboeuf, the night concierge, also found strangled in the kitchen cloakroom. An anonymous letter, apparently from Charlotte, has revealed Donge's connection with Mimi.

Maigret is convinced of his innocence; he also thinks Clark is not the killer. However a bank manager comes forward and tells Maigret that Donge had 300,000 francs in the bank, which came from Detroit.

Maigret questions a witness

Michael Gambon, Jack Galloway

Michael Gambon, Nicola Duffett

When Maigret learns that Jean Ramuel, a forger, had worked at the bank; he learned about Mimi Clark's relationship with Donge and sent her blackmail letters.

Ramuel, spotting her in the kitchen and fearing her appointment with Donge-who only wanted to see his son-killed her, knowing Donge would be blamed. He killed the night concierge, who saw him, and sent the anonymous letter he'd forged from Charlotte. He was about to escape to Brussels when Maigret catches up with him.

Scene in the meat locker

Jack Galloway, Michael J. Jackson, Michael Gambon

Toyah Willcox, Nicola Duffett

John Kavanagh, Michael Gambon

Toyah Willcox, Geoffrey Hutchings

John Moffatt, Michael Gambon

MAIGRET ON THE DEFENSIVE SEASON 2 EPISODE 3

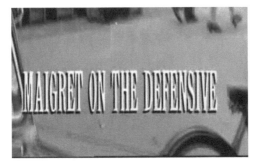

DIRECTED BY Stuart Burge ORIGINAL AIR DATE: 3/28/93

CAST

Michael Gambon..Inspector Jules Maigret
Barbara Flynn...............Madame Maigret
Geoffrey Hutchings...........Sergeant Lucas
Jack Galloway................Inspector Janvier
James Larkin...............Inspector Lapointe
Oliver Ford Davies..................Dr. Pardon
John Benfield......................Henri Lautier
Pip Torrens..............Chief Commissioner
John Cater..Porter
Deborah Findlay.................Juliette Motte
John Salthouse.................Francois Melan
Peter Kertesz....................................Desire
Liza Walker.........................Nicole Prieur
Susannah Doyle.....................Marguerite
James Saxon.....................Marcel Landry
Lajos Menzei........................Night Porter
Bella Tanay............................Manageress

Michael Gambon   Barbara Flynn   Geoffrey Hutchings

Jack Galloway   James Larkin   Oliver Ford Davies

John Benfield   Pip Torrens   John Cater

Deborah Findlay   John Salthouse   Liza Walker

Susannah Doyle   James Saxon   Lajos Menzei   Bella Tanay   Vegetable Seller   Woman

77

Maigret's doctor tells him he needs to take things easier. That night, answering a desperate phone call from a young lady in distress, Maigret meets the young woman in a bar. Since she has no money, The detective checks her into a respectable hotel and returns home to complete his interrupted night's sleep. He also has some restaurant thieves on his mind.

Dr. Milan's sign

John Benfield, Susannah Doyle

Michael Gambon as Maigret

When he reports to work, he finds that the young woman has concocted a charge of attempted rape and finds himself the subject of disciplinary action.

Maigret suspects his pursuit of a gang of restaurant thieves is the impetus for this accusation and with the help of his loyal staff, he is able to find the ultimate answer in a dentist's chair.

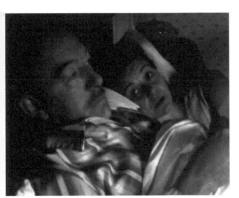

Michael Gambon, Barbara Flynn

Michael Gambon, Jack Galloway

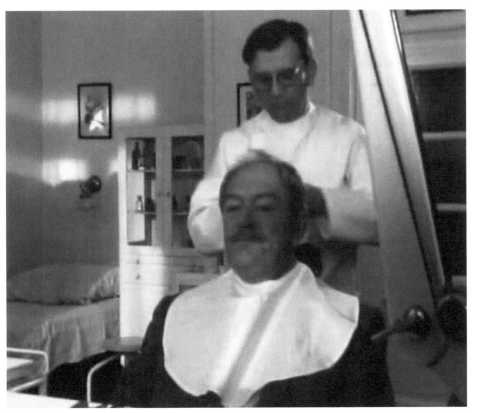

Is Maigret getting a haircut?

Although the Chief Commissioner has Maigret on the carpet-and warns him not to tell anyone else about the charges, he does tell Lucas, who in turns tells Janvier and Lapointe.

Geoffrey Hutchings, Michael Gambon

TV Poster

John Benfield, Michael Gambon

Pip Torrens making a point

Geoffrey Hutchings, James Larkin

Old Man, John Benfield

Maigret gets some help from Henri Lautier-whom he had suspected of being involved in the restaurant robberies. Henri and his girlfriend Marguerite noticed the accusing woman, Nicole Prieur, at the dentist's office across the street.

John Benfield, Michael Gambon

John Benfield in the market

Geoffrey Hutchings, Michael Gambon

Michael Gambon, Jack Galloway

Maigret lighting his pipe

Jack Galloway, Geoffrey Hutchings

Television Poster

John Cater, Michael Gambon

Maigret solves a murder case, catches the insane killer, and gets an apology from the Chief Commissioner. Maigret is reinstated with full honours.

MAIGRET'S BOYHOOD FRIEND SEASON 2 EPISODE 4

DIRECTED BY John Strickland ORIGINAL AIR DATE: 4/4/93

CAST

Michael Gambon..Inspector Jules Maigret
Barbara Flynn...............Madame Maigret
Geoffrey Hutchings...........Sergeant Lucas
Jack Galloway................Inspector Janvier
James Larkin...............Inspector Lapointe
Edward Petherbridge.........Leon Florentin
Kenneth Haigh....................Victor Drouet
Peter Blythe...................Fernand Courcel
Betty Marsden..........................Concierge
Alan David..........................Francois Pare
Peter-Hugo Daly.............Jean-Luc Bodard

Michael Gambon   Barbara Flynn   Geoffrey Hutchings

Jack Galloway   James Larkin   Edward Petherbridge

Kenneth Haigh   Peter Blythe   Betty Marsden

Alan David   Peter-Hugo Daly

Leon Florentin, an old school ac-
quaintance of Maigret, shows up at
the detective's home asking for help
in the shooting death of his mistress.

83

Maigret has only obvious distaste for the unkempt, disheveled Leon, who has survived since boyhood by sponging, lying, and conning his way through life.

Although the dead woman allowed him to live with her rent free, her busy social life included four other lovers, all of whom were unaware of the other's existence.

MAIGRET'S BOYHOOD FRIEND

TV Poster

Barbara Flynn, Michael Gambon

Michael Gambon, Edward Petherbridge

James Larkin, Michael Gambon

Edward Petherbridge, James Larkin

When they were scheduled to arrive, Leon would discreetly leave the apartment, but if they arrived unexpectedly, he would perversely hide in the wardrobe.

The plot becomes even more complicated when Maigret finds out that Leon was in the wardrobe when the murder was allegedly committed. One by one, Maigret and his team find and interview the other four men in the case.

Peter Blythe interrogated

Barbara Flynn, Michael Gambon

Geoffrey Hutchings as Lucas

Edward Petherbridge needs protection

Geoffrey Hutchings, Peter-Hugo Daly

James Larkin has a snack

Along with Florentin, Maigret assembles the other four men in his office. He announces that he believes one of them is the killer. He says that he also believes that one of the group knows who the murderer is.

Later, Maigret discovers that Leon was a blackmailer; the killer wanted some letters that he had written to the victim, that Florentin got hold of. Maigret also figures out who the killer is.

Jack Galloway, Edward Petherbridge, Michael Gambon

Alan David, Geoffrey Hutchings, Peter-Hugo Daly

Edward Petherbridge, Barbara Flynn

Peter Blythe, Kenneth Haigh, Alan David

Kenneth Haigh is a suspect

Edward Petherbridge, Peter Blythe

Peter Blythe, Kenneth Haigh

Geoffrey Hutchings passing a paper

Jack Galloway as Janvier

Maigret realizes that there was only one man who was rich enough for Leon to blackmail. Leon says that he has admitted to blackmail, but won't take the rap for a murder another man committed. Case solved.

MAIGRET & THE MINISTER SEASON 2 EPISODE 5

DIRECTED BY Nicholas Renton ORIGINAL AIR DATE: 4/11/93

CAST

Michael Gambon..Inspector Jules Maigret
Barbara Flynn................Madame Maigret
Geoffrey Hutchings...........Sergeant Lucas
Jack Galloway................Inspector Janvier
James Larkin...............Inspector Lapointe
Peter Barkworth....................The Minister
Jon Finch....................Charles Mascoulin
John Moffatt............................Comeliau
Sorcha Cusack...............Blanche Lamotte
Shaughan Seymour...........Jacques Fleury
Paul Gregory....................................Talbot
Michael Melia............................Catroux
David Glover....................Arthur Nicoud
John Hartley.................................Benoit
Jane Wymark.................Madame Gaudry
Eileen Page....................Madame Calame
Michael Melman........................Barman
Sandor Teri...............................Piquemal
Ferenc Takacs.........................Chairman
Kati Marton................Distraught Mother

Michael Gambon   Barbara Flynn   Geoffrey Hutchings

Jack Galloway   James Larkin   Peter Barkworth

Jon Finch   John Moffatt   Sorcha Cusack

Shaughan Seymour   Paul Gregory   Michael Melia

David Glover   John Hartley   Jane Wymark   Eileen Page   Michael Melman   Sandor Teri   Kati Marton

89

Man 1   Man 2   Man 3   Restaurant Patron   Security Man 1   Security Man 2   Woman 1

Woman 2

Maigret is called in the middle of the night by the Minister of Public Works to discreetly conduct an unofficial investigation into the theft of an engineering report from his office.

The paper was written years earlier and correctly predicted the collapse of a sanatorium which killed 62 children. The report by a Professor Julien Calame, an expert on applied mechanics and civil engineering, has never been published and nobody knows where it is.

Michael Gambon, Peter Barkworth

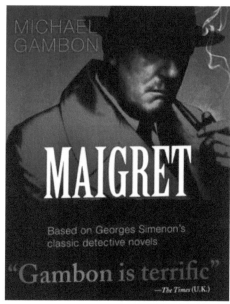

Michael Melia, Geoffrey Hutchings

Television Poster

Lucas holds up the newspaper

Michael Gambon, Jon Finch

Michael Gambon, Jack Galloway,
Geoffrey Hutchings

Peter Barkworth as the Minister

The team discusses the case over a meal

Jack Galloway, Michael Gambon

The high death toll puts everything and everyone connected with the building's construction under suspicion and the resultant scrutiny threatens to topple the government. Maigret correctly suspects the theft to be an inside job with politically-motivated ramifications.

A journalist is now suggesting that there are important people with something to hide. However, says the Minister, the report did exist and a man by the name of Piquemal, had given him a copy.

It concluded that the project was technically unsound and should be abandoned. Unfortunately, the report had been stolen from his apartment on the evening of the same day he had received it.

Michael Gambon, Michael Melia

TV Poster

Barbara Flynn, Michael Gambon

Michael Gambon, John Moffatt

Peter Barkworth as the Minister

As Maigret begins his investigation, which requires all of his team, he is soon aware that the Sûreté National is involved. There is also a suggestion that Arthur Nicoud who built the sanatorium, is trying to ensure that the report stays hidden.

Maigret realizes that the Calame Report is vital; he must at least discover who stole it if he cannot find the report itself. Maigret knows that the investigation is becoming a race against time as questions raised by newspapers are pressuring him.

Peter Barkworth, Michael Gambon

Michael Gambon, Peter Barkworth

Jon Finch looking angry

Having employed Lucas, Janvier and Lapointe full time, Maigret gathers much information, after which it is time to take action based on what has been deduced. The outcome, when it arrives, is both sudden and surprising.

Shaughan Seymour, Michael Gambon

Maigret with his team

Michael Gambon as Inspector Maigret

MAIGRET & THE MAID SEASON 2 EPISODE 6

DIRECTED BY Stuart Burge ORIGINAL AIR DATE: 4/18/93

CAST

Michael Gambon..Inspector Jules Maigret
Geoffrey Hutchings...........Sergeant Lucas
Jack Galloway................Inspector Janvier
James Larkin...............Inspector Lapointe
Susie Lindeman.............................Felice
Tony Rohr.............................Ernest Lapie
Paul Moriarty..............Inspector Bonneau
Ann Heffernan..............Madame Chochoi
Agnes Margitay..............................Louise
Steven Mackintosh.........Jacques Petillon
Ralph Nossek..............................Forrentin
Gregory Cox.................................Lepape
Miklos Lukacsi.................................Priest
Edward Tudor-Pole........................Pascal
Christopher Ryan...........................Basie
Barbara Hegyi.................................Nurse
Nick Lucas.........................Police Sergeant
Frigyes Mollosi........................Detective

Michael Gambon   Geoffrey Hutchings   Jack Galloway

James Larkin   Susie Lindeman   Tony Rohr

Paul Moriarty   Ann Heffernan   Agnes Margitay

Steven Mackintosh   Ralph Nossek   Gregory Cox

Miklos Lukacsi   Edward Tudor-Pole Christopher Ryan   Barbara Hegyi   Frigyes Mollosi   Boy   Girl

Man   Nurse   Policeman

Maigret is called in to investigate the murder of a one-legged retired clerk nicknamed "Pegleg," who was found shot to death at close range in the bedroom of his house in a small provincial town.

Maigret questions the middle-aged man's maid, an eccentric, irreverent, independent and irascible young woman named Felice. She dresses flamboyantly and refuses to be described as an employee of the dead man.

Maigret examines the gun

Susie Lindeman, Michael Gambon

Policeman, Paul Moriarty

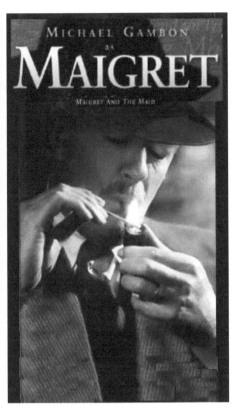

Geoffrey Hutchings, Michael Gambon

TV Poster

Barbara Hegyi, Michael Gambon, Susie Lindeman

Trumpet Player at the club

James Larkin with a witness

She is reluctant to co-operate with the inspector's inquiries; she is openly unpleasant to Maigret and keeps a secret diary where she writes longingly about her lover and their reunions.

Her exact relationship with the victim is unclear and she, along with the dead man's brother and saxophonist nephew, become suspects. Maigret's insight into human nature proves all this as fantasy.

Felice is merely a lonely and romantic young woman who wants more excitement than her provincial life as a servant can offer. Despite her hostility, Maigret comes to like her, and she begins to open up.

The dead man's relatives include a married brother who dislikes the girl, and a young nephew, a jazz saxophonist, who comes down from Paris for the funeral.

Period car in location scene

Steven Mackintosh on saxophone

Maigret reads a book

Steven Mackintosh, Agnes Margitay,
Tony Rohr

TV Poster

Mourners follow the funeral coach

Michael Gambon, Paul Moriarty

Geoffrey Hutchings on the phone

Michael Gambon, Geoffrey Hutchings

Most of the locals dislike Felice, however the shopkeeper backs up her alibi. Of course, she could be involved in the murder even if she was not present when the man was shot.

Maigret meets nephew Jacques Petillon outside the jazz club; Petillon is shot and taken to hospital. The assailant escapes. Meanwhile, someone breaks in and beats up Felice. She couldn't see who it was.

Maigret is able to solve the murder case; a friend of Jacques, who stole a large sum of money, hid it in the house, then was sent to prison. When he returned for it, Pegleg surprised him and was shot dead.

Jack Galloway on the phone

Michael Gambon, Susie Lindeman

Michael Gambon as Maigret

MAIGRET SETS A TRAP (2016)

Maigret Sets a Trap

DIRECTED BY ASHLEY PEARCE

CAST

Rowan Atkinson...Inspector Jules Maigret
Leo Staar.....................Inspector LaPointe
Shaun Dingwall.............Inspector Janvier
Lucy Cohu.....................Madame Maigret
Fiona Shaw....................Madame Moncin
Aidan McArdle................Judge Comeliau
Alexander Campbell..........Dennis Lecoin
Rufus Wright....................Minister Morel
David Dawson.................Marcel Moncin
Beth Cooke....................Georgette Lecoin
Eva-Jane Willis.............Marthe Jusserand
Zsofia Rea...........................Nicole Lecoin
Colin Mace....................Inspector Lognon
Hugh Simon...............................Dr. Paul
Leo Hatton................................Michelle
Ian Bartholomew.......................The Baron
Katie Lyons....................Madame Maguy
Jack Johns.............................Rougin
Christopher Bowen.........Inspector Lefors
Heather Bleasdale..........Madame Pardon
Gillian Bevan...................Madame Tissot
Rebecca Night.................Yvonne Moncin
Jessica Bay...............................Odile
Martin Turner..........................Dr. Pardon
David Annen...................Professor Tissot
Jack McMullen..............................Mazet
Mark Heap.......................................Moers

Rowan Atkinson   Leo Staar   Shaun Dingwall

Lucy Cohu   Fiona Shaw   Aidan McArdle

Alexander Campbell   Rufus Wright   David Dawson

Beth Cooke   Eva-Jane Willis   Zsofia Rea

Colin Mace   Hugh Simon   Leo Hatton

Renny Krupinski..........................Boniek
Matt Devere....................Police Inspector
Scott Alexander Young..............Inspector
Ede Pszotka.........................Delivery Boy
Nick Wittman....................................Lad

Ian Bartholomew   Katie Lyons   Christopher Bowen

Heather Bleasdale   Gillian Bevan   Rebecca Night   Jessica Bay   Martin Turner   David Annen   Jack McMullen

Mark Heap   Renny Krupinski   Matt Devere

Over a five month period in 1955 four women are stabbed to death in Montmartre after dark, a prostitute and a midwife among them - women with nothing in common beyond being brunette.

Rowan Atkinson, Shaun Dingwall

Shaun Dingwall, Leo Staar

Justice minister Morel leans on chief Inspector Maigret to catch the murderer and Maigret sets a trap, using policewoman Marthe Jusserard as a decoy. She survives an attack, sartorial evidence leading to married mother's boy Marcel Moncin, whom Maigret arrests.

However whilst Moncin is in custody there is a further murder and Maigret looks to Moncin's family to help solve the murders. Has Maigret got the wrong man or does Moncin have an accomplice?

Maigret with period car

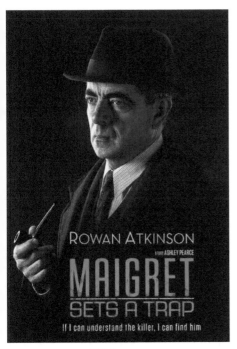

TV Poster

Rowan Atkinson, Rebecca Night

David Dawson, Rowan Atkinson

Eva-Jane Willis, Rowan Atkinson

Maigret is certain that Moncin is crazy; he even tells him that he will wind up in a lunatic asylum. Moncin adamantly denies being insane; his mother tells Maigret to release Marcel.

Finally, Moncin admits that he killed the women. Since nobody thought he could possibly be a killer, he decided to prove them wrong. Moncin's wife admits to killing the other woman while her husband was in jail.

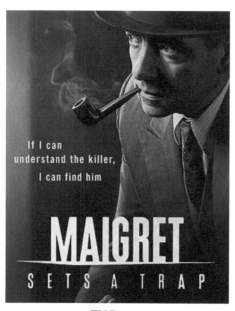

TV Poster

Rowan Atkinson as Maigret

Leo Staar, Rowan Atkinson

MAIGRET'S DEAD MAN (2016)

Maigret's Dead Man

DIRECTED BY Jon East

CAST

Rowan Atkinson...Inspector Jules Maigret
Leo Staar.....................Inspector LaPointe
Shaun Dingwall..............Inspector Janvier
Lucy Cohu....................Madame Maigret
Aidan McArdle...............Judge Comeliau
Ian Puleston-Davies.......Inspector Colombani
Dorrottya Hais............................Nicole
Mark Hadfield..................Albert Rochain
Ivan Fenyo...........................Pietr
Denes Bernath...............Victor Poliensky
Mark Heap.................Dr. Moers
Hugh Simon.......................Dr. Paul
Ann Queensberry..............Claire Fontaine
John Light...............................Dacourt
Michael Fitzgerald.........Hotel Proprietor
Anamaria Marinca.........................Maria
Amber Anderson........................Francine
Gabi Fon..................................Adele
Ross Waiton.................................Bargee
Ralph Burkin.............................Landlord
Nathalie Armin..............................Nina
Tim Chipping..........................Boxer Joe
Matt Devere.............................Detective
Grant Simpson............................Barman
Oengus MacNamara...............Bookamker
Karen Gagnon.............Police Telephonist
Russell Dean.................Post Office Clerk

Rowan Atkinson   Leo Staar   Shaun Dingwall

Lucy Cohu   Aidan McArdle   Ian Puleston-Davies

Dorrottya Hais   Mark Hadfield   Ivan Fenyo

Denes Bernath   Mark Heap   Hugh Simon

Ann Queensberry   John Light   Michael Fitzgerald

Katia Bokor.......................................Nurse
Philip Benjamin.........................Interpreter
Livia Habermann..........................Midwife
Peter Schueller..............................Reveller

Anamaria Marinca   Amber Anderson   Nathalie Armin

Tim Chipping   Matt Devere   Grant Simpson   Oengus MacNamara   Karen Gagnon   Katia Bokor   Peter Schueller

88 minutes

Maigret's officers are called upon to assist in the case of three vicious murders at farm houses in Picardy; the news hits the national headlines and the elite Brigade Criminelle at the Quay Des Orfevres is called upon to lend its expertise in tracking down the brutal gang responsible for the slaughter.

TV Poster

Maigret reads a George Simenon book

Maigret is intrigued when a man phoning him to say he fears he is about to be killed and calling himself only 'Nina's husband' is indeed found slain.

A witness appeal identifies him as café owner Albert Rochain, whose killers seemed to be looking for something and by reopening the café Maigret attracts a suspect, Victor Poliensky, and can identify his accomplices, apparently connecting Albert to the Picardy killers.

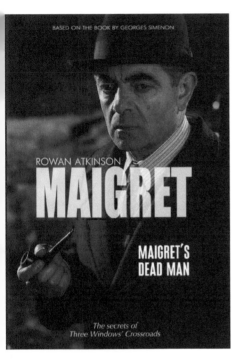

TV Poster

Rowan Atkinson & Lucy Cohu

Rowan Atkinson, Leo Staar

Shaun Dingwall taking aim

Shaun Dingwall & Rowan Atkinson

This is confirmed when a female gang member survives an attack by another of the killers, shot dead by Maigret. Inspector Maigret is resolute in investigating the murder of the obscure anonymous Parisian, an investigation that ultimately solves both crimes.

Ultimately a newspaper advert results in a friend of Albert linking him to a gang of race course fixers, which in turn leads to the identity of the leader of the Picardy murderers, and the closure of the cases.

Rowan Atkinson, Ian Puleston-Davies

Lucy Cohu, Rowan Atkinson

Rowan Atkinson, Ian Puleston-Davies

MAIGRET: NIGHT AT THE CROSSROADS (2017)

Maigret's Night at the Crossroads

DIRECTED BY Sarah Harding
CAST

Rowan Atkinson...Inspector Jules Maigret
Leo Staar....................Inspector LaPointe
Shaun Dingwall..............Inspector Janvier
Lucy Cohu....................Madame Maigret
Aidan McArdle................Judge Comeliau
Kevin McNally..........Inspector Grandjean
Jonathan Newth........Ambassador Sievens
Tom Wlaschhiha...............Carl Andersson
Mia Jexen.........................Else Andersson
Ben Caplan.......................Isaac Goldberg
Katherine Kanter..............Sarah Goldberg
Robin Weaver...........Madame Michonnet
Wanda Opalinska...........................Jo Jo
Stephen Wright...............Thierry Bertinet
Mark Heap......................................Moers
Paul Chahidi............................Michonnet
Chook Sibtain..................................Oscar
Dorothy Atkinson..........Claire Grandjean
Max Wrottesley.........................Wilmotts
Bjorn Freiberg.........Antwerp Card Player

Rowan Atkinson   Leo Staar   Shaun Dingwall

Lucy Cohu   Aidan McArdle   Kevin McNally

Jonathan Newth   Tom Wlaschhiha   Mia Jexen

Ben Caplan   Katherine Kanter   Robin Weaver

Wanda Opalinska   Stephen Wright   Mark Heap   Paul Chahidi   Chook Sibtain   Dorothy Atkinson   Max Wrottesley

Bjorn Freiberg

88 minites

Jeweller Isaac Goldberg leaves Antwerp with a cache of stolen diamonds but his body is found in the French village of Arpajon in a car belonging to aloof Dane Carl Andersson.

Maigret has been interrogating the mysterious Dane for hours without a confession. Why was the body of a diamond merchant found in his car at his isolated mansion?

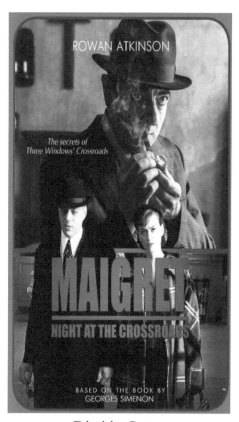

Television Poster

Maigret mulling the case

Shaun Dingwall, Rowan Atkinson,
Leo Staar

Shaun Dingwall, Stephen Wight, Rowan
Atkinson, Kevin McNally

Mia Jexen, Kevin McNally,
Rowan Atkinson

Rowan Atkinson
Maigret's Night at the Crossroads

TV Film Poster

Vitamin pills, or something else?

He's either innocent or a very good liar. Other villagers dislike him, telling Maigret he keeps his sister Else locked in her room and, whilst protesting his innocence, Carl attempts suicide when Maigret discovers that there are no records of his existence. What does his beautiful but vulnerable sister know? And what compels everyone at the Three Widows Crossroads to be so secretive? Maigret releases him in the hopes that he will lead him to the missing diamonds and the actual murderer.

The death of another suspect causes Maigret to believe the killer is one of the other villagers working in collusion with a member of the police force. Maigret sets out to find his killer which ultimately leads to a thrilling climax.

Rowan Atkinson as Maigret

Maigret with his pipe

Mia Jexen, Tom Wlaschiha

MAIGRET IN MONTMARTRE (2017)

DIRECTED BY Thaddeus O'Sullivan

CAST

Rowan Atkinson...Inspector Jules Maigret
Leo Staar....................Inspector LaPointe
Shaun Dingwall..............Inspector Janvier
Lucy Cohu....................Madame Maigret
Nicola Sloane.....................The Countess
Olivia Vinall...................................Arlette
Adrian Rawlins..............Oscar Bonvoisin
Douglas Hodge....................Fred Alfonsi
Sebastian De Souza.......Philippe Martinot
Simon Gregor.......................Grasshopper
Lorraine Ashbourne.............Rosa Alfonsi
Cassie Clare.....................................Tania
Colin Mace....................Inspector Lognon
Hugh Simon...............................Dr. Paul
Adrian Scarborough..................Dr. Bloch
Mark Heap................................Dr. Moers
Nike Kurta..Betty
Jane Wood.......................Madame Aubin
Sara Kestelman.........Madame Dussardier
Tilly Vosburgh............Nathalie Moncoeur
Alexandra Bakonyi...................Genevieve
Gyula Mesterhazy..............Man at Pissoir

Rowan Atkinson · Leo Staar · Shaun Dingwall

Lucy Cohu · Nicola Sloane · Olivia Vinall

Adrian Rawlins · Douglas Hodge · Sebastian De Souza

Simon Gregor · Lorraine Ashbourne · Cassie Clare

Colin Mace · Adrian Scarborough · Nike Kurta

Sara Kestelman   Tilly Vosburgh   Gyula Mesterhazy

90 minutes

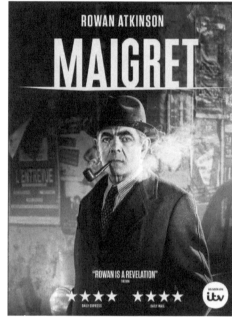

After telling Maigret she over-
heard a plot to kill 'the countess,'
club singer Arlette is strangled and
soon afterwards the body of an elderly, reclusive countess is also discovered.

Rowan Atkinson questions a suspect

Television Poster

Leo Staar, Rowan Atkinson, Shaun Dingwall

Inspector Maigret on the phone

Sara Kestelman, Rowan Atkinson

Maigret sits, but cannot relax

Maigret believes a third person was present when Arlette was killed and is anxious to trace a man called Oscar, whose name Arlette cried out in her sleep.

Meanwhile young rent boy Philippe, who shared the countess's drug addiction, survives an attempt on his life but is too scared to help the police.

Maigret finds out that both the dead women once lived at a Nice hotel, where the countess's husband died in odd circumstances and where Oscar also worked.

This leads him to track down Oscar and to the close of his case. Maigret discovers a dark secret that links their past lives at the Grand Hotel in Nice.

Rowan Atkinson, Simon Gregor

Rowan Atkinson as Maigret

Maigret out on a snowy day

Lorraine Ashbourne, Rowan Atkinson

Lightning Source UK Ltd.
Milton Keynes UK
UKHW051528120223
416655UK00015B/10